2   Fuel and energy foods, to help you to think and to work:

Sugary and starchy foods such as bread and potatoes, and those containing fats like butter and margarine, and dairy foods.

3   Protective foods, to protect your body against some illnesses, and to control your body processes:

Protective foods include those that supply vitamins and mineral elements: oranges for example, and green vegetables.

It should be remembered that most dishes are a mixture of foods from all three groups, and so contain more than one particular nutrient.

Contents

Acknowledgments

The author and publishers wish to acknowledge the help of EMGAS, Leicester (the cooker); Hardy & Co (Furnishers) Ltd, Loughborough (dining furniture); Spectrum Fabrics, Loughborough and Ashby de la Zouch (background materials); and Wrighton International Furniture, London (kitchen units) in the production of photographs for this book.

Easy Meals

by LYNNE PEEBLES
photographs by TIM CLARK

Ladybird Books Loughborough

SIMPLE COLD SNACKS

Based on bread

Preparation time, 5–10 minutes

Buy some long dinner rolls, and cut almost through to make slits.
The slits can be filled with two or more of the following:

1 Grated cheese mixed with pickle.

2 Cottage cheese mixed with chopped chives (add salt and pepper to taste).

3 Hard-boiled eggs, chopped and mixed with mayonnaise (add salt and pepper to taste).

4 Hard-boiled eggs mixed with chopped cress (add salt and pepper to taste).

5 Canned tuna, prawns, shrimps or salmon mixed with a little lemon juice, salt and pepper, and chopped skinned tomato.

Any or all of the above can be garnished with onion rings, shredded lettuce, and sliced cucumber.

Open sandwiches

Using bread (brown or white) or crispbread as a base, top with a mixture of salad ingredients and fruit plus cheese, meat, eggs or fish.

Serve with a dressing, and set a knife and fork.

Simple French dressing

Preparation time, 2 minutes

INGREDIENTS

2 tablespoonfuls corn oil
Salt and pepper
Pinch dry mustard
3 tablespoonfuls vinegar
1 tablespoonful lemon juice

Place all ingredients in a screw-topped jar, and shake well.

HOT SNACKS *Based on bread*

Three-decker club sandwiches

Cooking time, 5 minutes
Preparation time, 5 minutes

INGREDIENTS
3 slices bread
50 g (2 oz) butter
50 g (2 oz) cheese
1 slice cooked ham
Mayonnaise
Pickle
Lettuce and tomato

1 Toast and butter bread.
2 On one slice, place ham and a little mayonnaise.
3 Top with second slice of toast.
4 Cover second slice with grated cheese and a little pickle.
5 Top with third slice of toast, butter side down.
6 Cut into four cross-wise, and top with quarters of tomato.
7 Serve while still warm, with lettuce.

Grilled or oven-baked rolls

Preparation time, 5–10 minutes, cooking time 15 minutes

INGREDIENTS

A 2 round rolls
   1 small onion
   1 rasher bacon
   25 g (1 oz) butter
   2 eggs
   1 tomato
   Pepper

B 2 round rolls
   $12\frac{1}{2}$ g ($\frac{1}{2}$ oz) butter
   1 small onion
   50 g (2 oz) grated cheese
   Chopped parsley
   Salt and pepper

For filling A

1 Peel and chop onion finely. Remove rind and chop bacon finely.

2 Lightly fry bacon in butter with onion and pepper until just soft.

3 Place in hollow centre of roll.

4 Break egg into centre.

5 Top with sliced tomato.

6 Wrap loosely in foil, place on baking tray and bake in centre of moderate oven Gas Mark 4 (electricity 350°F/180°C) for 15 minutes.

EQUIPMENT

Chopping board
Sharp knife
Baking sheet
Grater
Foil

Cut a slice from the rounded top of each roll, and slightly hollow out centre of roll.

8

For filling B

1 Peel and finely chop onion. Mix with grated cheese, butter, egg, parsley, and salt and pepper.

2 Fill hollow in rolls, and put top back on. Wrap in foil and bake in centre of a moderate oven Gas Mark 4 (electricity 350°F/180°C) for 15 minutes.

Omelettes

Preparation and cooking time, 10–15 minutes

Plain Omelette – basic recipe

INGREDIENTS
For each person:
2 eggs
Salt and pepper
1 tablespoonful water
12½ g (½ oz) butter

EQUIPMENT
Small omelette
(or frying) pan
Palette knife
Fork – Small basin

1 Break eggs into a small basin, and add salt, pepper and water. Beat with a fork to mix together.

2 Place butter in pan and heat to melt, tilting pan to ensure base is evenly covered.

3 Pour in egg mixture, and leave to set for one minute.

4 Using palette knife to draw in sides, tilt pan to allow mixture to spread evenly and set.

5 When set fold in half or into thirds, using a palette knife. Turn onto a hot plate and serve.

Variations

Ham and Onion Omelette

Add 25 g (1 oz) of chopped cooked ham, 1 small finely chopped onion and a pinch of dry mustard to egg mixture before cooking.

Mushroom Omelette

Wash and slice 50 g (2 oz) mushrooms, and fry in 25 g (1 oz) butter before adding egg mixture to pan.

Cheese Omelette

Make as for plain omelette, but sprinkle cooked omelette with 50 g (2 oz) of grated cheese before folding.

As-you-like-it Omelette

INGREDIENTS
25 g (1 oz) cooked peas
2 skinned and sliced tomatoes
25 g (1 oz) mushrooms
1 rasher bacon (remove rind and chop)
50 g (2 oz) cold cooked meat
1 small onion, finely chopped

1 Choose some or all of the above ingredients and fry gently in 25 g (1 oz) of butter before adding the egg mixture.

2 Allow base to set as before. Sprinkle top with 25–50 g (1–2 oz) grated cheese, and set top side under a hot grill.

Serve any of the omelettes with sliced tomato, crisps or bread and butter.

BREAKFASTS

The first meal of the day is very important, but it should not be one that involves a great deal of work early in the morning. Ideally, setting the table the night before and doing as much advance preparation as possible will help the mornings to run smoothly.

Muesli

Preparation time, 5 minutes

INGREDIENTS

4 tablespoonfuls rolled oats
50 g (2 oz) sultanas
25 g (1 oz) brown sugar or honey
A few chopped nuts
125 ml (¼ pint) milk
1 grated apple or 1 sliced banana
Some 'top of the milk'

1 Mix together the first five ingredients and leave in a cool place overnight.

2 To serve, add grated apple or chopped banana and a little 'top of the milk'.

Orange and grapefruit cocktail

INGREDIENTS
1 orange
1 grapefruit
12½g (½ oz) sugar (or to taste)

Preparation time,
10 minutes

1 Peel orange and grapefruit and remove all pith and segment skins.

2 Place segments and juice in a bowl.

3 Dissolve sugar in one tablespoonful water and pour over fruit. Chill and serve.

15

Grilled grapefruit

Preparation time, 5 minutes, plus 30 minutes standing time. Cooking time 2-3 minutes

INGREDIENTS

1 grapefruit, 25–40 g (1–1¾ oz) brown sugar

1 Cut grapefruit in half. Loosen and lift segments with a grapefruit knife, removing segment skins and centre.

2 Sprinkle with brown sugar. Leave for a minimum of half an hour (or overnight) in a cool place.

3 To serve, grill 2–3 minutes until sugar begins to darken slightly.

Quick hot dishes
Egg-bread and bacon

Preparation and cooking
time, 10 minutes

INGREDIENTS
1 egg
1 tablespoonful milk
1 piece bread (remove crusts)
1 rasher bacon
12½–25 g (½–1 oz) lard

1 Place bacon in pan with lard and fry gently.

2 Meanwhile place egg in small bowl with milk and beat
   well together.

3 Cut bread into four triangles and dip into egg.

4 Add to bacon and fry gently, turning once. Serve
   immediately.

Tomato toast

Preparation and cooking
time, 10 minutes

INGREDIENTS
1 piece bread
25 g (1 oz) butter
Marmite
2 skinned and sliced tomatoes

1 Heat grill.

2 Toast bread on one side, then lightly butter
   untoasted side and spread with Marmite.

3 Cover with sliced tomatoes. Grill until bubbly.

Preparation and cooking time, 20 minutes

MENU
Grilled grapefruit *or* Grapefruit and Orange cocktail (pages 15 and 16)
Egg, bacon, sausage and tomato
Toast and preserve – Tea

1 Set table or tray.

2 Melt 25g (1 oz) of lard in a frying pan.

3 Remove bacon rind. Pierce sausage skin.

4 Fry bacon and sausage gently for 3–4 minutes, turning once.

5 Add halved tomato sprinkled with pepper. Boil water for tea. Toast bread.

6 Add egg. Reduce heat. Fry gently until just firm.

7 Make tea. Serve toast.

8 Place sausage, egg, bacon and tomato on hot plate and serve meal.

Traditional English breakfast

19

SAVOURY DISHES

Mixed vegetable and chicken soup (for 3) *almost a meal in itself!*

INGREDIENTS
2 chicken stock cubes
1 uncooked chicken joint
1 onion   –   1 carrot
1 stick celery
50g (2 oz) spaghetti
100g (4 oz) cabbage
or green beans
2 tomatoes skinned
25g (1 oz) margarine
25g (1 oz) flour
Salt and pepper
250 ml ($\frac{1}{2}$ pint) milk
375 ml ($\frac{3}{4}$ pint) water

Preparation time, 5–10
minutes, cooking time,
35 minutes

*Shake pan gently over low
heat to sweat vegetables.*

1 Chop all vegetables.
Remove chicken from
bone, and chop. Place
together in a large covered
pan with margarine.
Sweat gently on a low heat
for 5 minutes, shaking
the pan often.

2 Add stock cubes, water,
salt, pepper and finely
broken spaghetti, also
chicken bones.

3 Bring to boil, reduce heat, and simmer for 30 minutes until vegetables are soft. Take out chicken bones.

4 Blend flour and milk together, and add to pan. Heat, and boil for 1 minute. Taste and re-season if needed.

Serve with fresh crusty bread.

Quick soup *Clear Vegetable*

Preparation time, 5 minutes, cooking time 15 minutes

INGREDIENTS

50 g (2 oz) peas	*1 stick celery very finely chopped*
1 grated onion	*12½ g (½ oz) butter or margarine*
1 grated carrot	*Seasoning 1 stock cube*

1 Place prepared vegetables in the base of a pan. Add margarine or butter and sweat vegetables gently in pan (with lid on) over low heat for 3 minutes.

2 Add 375 ml (¾ pint) water and stock cube.

3 Bring to boil. Reduce heat and simmer gently for 10 minutes. Season to taste and serve with toast.

Leek and ham au gratin (for 2)

Preparation time, 10–15 minutes, cooking time, 25 minutes

INGREDIENTS
4 leeks
4 slices cooked ham
25 g (1 oz) butter
25 g (1 oz) flour
250 ml ($\frac{1}{2}$ pint) milk
Salt and pepper
Pinch dry mustard
100 g (4 oz) grated cheese
1 slice bread

EQUIPMENT
Wooden spoon
Chopping board
Sharp knife
Pan
Grater
Shallow oven-proof dish

1 Cut off root and the green top to within $2\frac{1}{2}$ cm (1 inch) of the white stem on each leek. Wash very well in cold salt water.

2 Place in a pan of boiling salted water, cover, and simmer gently for 15 minutes until just tender. Test with pointed knife. Drain well.

SAUCE

3 Place butter in small pan and melt over a low heat. Add flour and, stirring all the time, cook for 1 minute.

4 Remove from heat and gradually stir in the milk.

5 Return to heat, and stirring all the time, bring to boil and boil for 1 minute until smooth and thick. Remove from heat, and season to taste adding mustard, salt, pepper, and 50 g (2 oz) of cheese.

6 Wrap each leek in a piece of ham, and place them in the base of a shallow oven-proof dish.

7 Spoon sauce on top, and sprinkle with remaining grated cheese.

8 Cut crusts off bread, cut bread into triangles and arrange around sides of dish.

9 To complete, either grill for 2–3 minutes or place in centre of a moderate oven, Gas Mark 4 (electricity 350°F/180°C) for 15 minutes until bubbling and brown.

Serve with potatoes.

Savoury liver (for 2)

Preparation and cooking time, 30–35 minutes

INGREDIENTS
150 g (6 oz) lamb's liver
2 rashers bacon
2 large tomatoes
50 g (2 oz) mushrooms
25 g (1 oz) flour
25 g (1 oz) lard
Salt and pepper
200 ml ($\frac{1}{3}$ pint) water
1 onion

EQUIPMENT
Shallow oven-proof dish
Frying pan
Fish slice
Wooden spoon

1 Peel onion and cut into rings, then fry gently in lard.

2 Cut rind off bacon and cut each piece in two. Skin
   tomatoes, and wash and slice mushrooms.

3 Keeping onion to one side of pan, add mushrooms and
   tomatoes. Fry for 30 seconds only. Transfer all pan
   ingredients to hot serving dish and arrange as border
   around edge.

4 Wash liver in cold salted water. Cut into thin strips.
   Add salt and pepper to flour, and coat liver.
   Fry liver and bacon for 5–8 minutes, turning once. Place
   in serving dish. Add remaining flour to pan. Cook gently,
   stirring for 1 minute. Add water gradually. Bring to boil.

stirring all the time until a thick gravy has been made. Taste and re-season. Serve separately.

If possible, with iron-rich foods like liver, always serve tomatoes as they contain vitamin C, which helps your body to absorb the iron.

Serve with potatoes and green vegetables.

Corned beef or ham hash (for 2)

Preparation time, 10 minutes, cooking time, 30 minutes

INGREDIENTS

*Small tin 250g (10 oz) corned beef or 250g (10 oz)
cooked ham – 1 egg – 25 g (1 oz) butter or dripping –
1 onion – Parsley – Salt and pepper*

*400g (1 lb) potatoes
50g (2 oz) butter
2 tablespoonfuls milk
Salt and pepper*

} *To make creamed potato (or
use 400g (1 lb) cooked
creamed potato)*

1 Peel and cook potatoes in salted water for approximately 20 minutes, then drain, add milk, salt and pepper, and mash well.

2 Add beaten egg to potato. Mix well.

3 Dice corned beef, finely chop onions.

4 Melt butter in frying pan and lightly fry onion.

5 Add potato and corned beef, and spread over base of pan. Cook until underside is brown and the mixture is really hot.

Garnish with parsley, and serve with assorted pickles.

Easy chicken savoury (for 2)

Preparation time, 10 minutes,
cooking time, 35–40 minutes

INGREDIENTS
2 chicken joints
50 g (2 oz) mushrooms
Salt and pepper
Small can of mushroom soup
(Crushed clove of garlic if liked)
Teaspoonful parsley
1 small chopped onion
12½ g (½ oz) flour
25 g (1 oz) lard or oil

1 Remove skin from chicken. Dip in flour, fry lightly in the base of a saucepan in the lard or oil with the onion, add salt and pepper (and crushed garlic if liked).

2 Fry gently 5 minutes each side until just brown.

3 Add sliced mushrooms and tin of soup.

4 Bring slowly to the boil, reduce heat and simmer (with lid on pan) until meat is tender – approximately 30 minutes.

Serve with a green vegetable and potatoes, and garnished with chopped parsley.

To vary the taste: Replace mushrooms and mushroom soup with 50 g (2 oz) peas and a small tin of vegetable soup.

To crush garlic: Remove skin, and roughly chop. Add half teaspoonful of salt and mix. Press with flat blade of sharp knife.

Lemon baked fish (for 2)

Preparation time, 10 minutes, cooking time, 20–35 minute

INGREDIENTS

2 fillets (or steaks) of white fish such as
*   cod, haddock, plaice or whiting*
1 slice bread
Salt and pepper
Juice of ½ lemon (use remaining half for serving)
1 small chopped onion
1 teaspoonful chopped parsley
50g (2 oz) butter

1 Wash fish, and peel and chop onion. Squeeze lemon, chop parsley and make bread into crumbs. Melt butter.

2 Mix breadcrumbs, lemon juice, chopped onion, salt and pepper together.

3 Lightly grease the base of a shallow oven-proof dish.

4 Place fish in base of dish (skin side down on fillets).

5 Top with stuffing mixture, spreading it over the whole of the fish. Pour over melted butter.

6 Bake at Gas Mark 5 (electricity 375°F/190°C) – 20 minutes for fillets, 30–35 for steaks. To test, push a pointed knife into the thickest part – it should go in and come out easily.

Serve with oven-baked tomatoes and peas.

Liver or chicken risotto

Preparation time, 10 minutes, cooking time, 30 minutes

INGREDIENTS

1 chicken joint or
100g (4 oz) lamb's liver
100g (4 oz) long grain
(Patna) rice
1 chicken stock cube
1 teaspoonful chopped
parsley
50g (2 oz) peas
(optional: 1 red or green
pepper and 50g (2 oz)
mushrooms)
375 ml (¾ pint) water
25g (1 oz) margarine
1 onion – 2 tomatoes
75–100g (3–4 oz) grated
cheese

1 Peel and chop onion, wash and chop liver, or skin chicken and remove meat from bones. Skin and chop tomatoes. (Wash, remove seeds and slice pepper, wash and slice mushrooms.) Grate cheese.

2 Melt margarine in pan, and lightly fry onion and liver (or chicken) to brown. Add rice and fry gently for 1 minute. Dissolve stock cube in water, then add remaining ingredients, except cheese.

3 Bring to boil, reduce heat and simmer for 20–25 minutes, until all liquid is absorbed, stirring occasionally. Sprinkle with cheese and serve.

To skin tomatoes
Spear on a fork, turn over hotplate or gas burner until skin pops. Remove skin.

Super sausage roll

Preparation time, 10 – 25 minutes,
cooking time, 40 minutes

INGREDIENTS

*200 g (8 oz) packet frozen
puff pastry OR shortcrust
pastry made from
200 g (8 oz) plain flour
50 g (2 oz) lard
50 g (2 oz) hard margarine
Pinch of salt
2½ –3 tablespoonfuls
cold water*

*Flour for rolling
200 g (8 oz) sausage meat
1 hardboiled egg
(chopped)
Teaspoonful of chopped
parsley (optional)
Salt and pepper
1 chopped onion
1 small beaten egg*

1 If making the pastry: sift the flour and salt, cut
   the fat into small pieces and rub it into the flour
   and salt with the fingertips (or use a fork) until
   the mixture looks like breadcrumbs. Add the
   water, and mix with a knife to a firm dough.

2 Roll out the pastry into a square approximately
   25 cm × 25 cm (10 in × 10 in).

3 Mix together the sausage meat, hardboiled egg, chopped parsley, salt, pepper and onion. Add approximately half the beaten egg, and mix well.

4 Place the sausage mixture in the centre of the pastry. Brush the edges of the pastry with water. To seal, roll over and tuck in the pastry ends.

5 Score the pastry lightly with a knife and brush with the remaining beaten egg. Decorate with any pastry trimmings.

6 Bake at Gas Mark 7 (electricity 425°F/220°C) for 20 minutes. Reduce the heat to Gas Mark 4 (electricity 350°F/180°C) and continue cooking for another 20 minutes. Cover with foil to prevent over browning.

7 Serve hot with a green vegetable and potatoes, or cold with a seasonal salad.
This dish is ideal for a picnic, either packed whole or in slices.

HOW TO COOK VEGETABLES

Vegetables are protective foods and form an important part of a balanced diet. They must, however, be cooked correctly in order to retain their nutritional value. This quick reference chart shows some interesting ways to prepare different types of vegetables, to make them attractive to look at and delicious to eat.

VEGETABLE	PREPARATION	COOKING	SERVING
Creamed Potatoes 400 g (1 lb) potatoes 50 g (2 oz) butter 3 tbsps milk Salt and pepper	1 Wash, peel and cut into even-sized pieces. 2 Place in a pan of cold salt water.	1 Bring to the boil, reduce the heat and simmer for 20 minutes until just soft. 2 Drain, mash, then add butter, milk and pepper.	Garnish with parsley.
Potato Croquettes 400 g (1 lb) potatoes 25 g (1 oz) butter Salt and pepper 1 egg 1 egg (beaten) Brown breadcrumbs Fat for deep frying Flour	As above	1 As above, adding an egg at stage 2. Cool. 2 On a floured board, shape into small rolls. Dip each roll first in beaten egg, then in breadcrumbs, then repeat this. (This prevents breaking.) 3 Deep fry in hot fat for 3-4 minutes. Drain well.	Serve immediately. Garnish with parsley.
Sauté Potatoes 400 g (1 lb) potatoes 75 g (3 oz) butter 3 tbsps corn oil Salt and pepper	As above	1 Bring to the boil, reduce the heat and simmer for 5-7 minutes only. Drain. Cool. Cut into slices. 2 Melt the butter and oil in a frying pan. Add the potato slices and fry until golden brown on both sides.	Place in a serving dish. Sprinkle with salt, pepper and parsley.
Baked Potatoes 1 medium potato per person 25-50 g (1-2 oz) butter Salt and pepper	1 Scrub the potatoes very well. 2 Prick with a fork all over. 3 Roll in salt and place on a baking tray.	Bake at Gas Mark 6 (electricity 400°F/200°C) for approximately 1 hour (depending on the size) in the centre of the oven until the centres are soft when a knife is inserted.	Cut a cross in the top of each potato. Sprinkle with salt and pepper, add butter to taste

Oven-baked Tomatoes 4 tomatoes 25 g (1 oz) butter Salt and pepper	1 Wash the tomatoes and place in an ovenproof dish. 2 Make two slits in the top of each tomato. 3 Top with a knob of butter and sprinkle with salt and pepper.	Bake in the centre of the oven for 15-20 minutes on Gas Mark 4-5 (electricity 350°F/180°C — 375°F/190°C)	Sprinkle with parsley.
Carrots 200 g (8 oz) carrots 50 g (2 oz) butter ½ level teasp salt Level teasp sugar	1 Peel or scrape the carrots. Wash. 2 Slice thinly and place in cold salt water with sugar.	Bring to the boil, reduce the heat and simmer for 15-20 minutes until just soft. Drain.	Serve with butter and parsley.
Brussels Sprouts 200 g (8 oz) sprouts 25 g (1 oz) butter Salt	1 Remove the outer leaves. 2 Make a cross in the base of each stem with a knife. Wash well.	Place in boiling salt water. Cook for ten minutes. Drain.	Serve with butter.
Green Beans 200 g (8 oz) beans 25 g (1 oz) butter Salt	1 Top, tail and string beans. Slice thinly (small ones may be left whole.) Wash.	Cook in boiling salt water until just soft for 8-10 minutes. Drain.	Toss in melted butter and sprinkle with salt and pepper before serving.
Broccoli 400 g (1 lb) broccoli 25 g (1 oz) butter Teasp salt	Select fresh white or purple headed. Use the head plus 7½-10 cm (3-4") of stalk. Wash very well.	Place in boiling salt water for 10-15 minutes until just soft.	Serve with butter.
Ratatouille 1 onion 1 clove of garlic 50 g (2 oz) butter 1 medium aubergine 100 g (4 oz) courgettes 1 small green pepper 3 skinned tomatoes ½ level teasp salt 1 tbsp parsley	1 Peel and thinly slice the onion. 2 Remove the skin of the garlic and crush the garlic with salt. *(See page 29)* 3 Slice the aubergine and courgettes thinly. 4 De-seed, slice and chop the pepper. 5 Chop the tomatoes and the parsley.	1 Fry the onion with butter and garlic for 4-5 minutes. 2 Add the remaining ingredients to the pan. Cover and cook until just soft.	Serve with any red meat dish.
Corn on the cob 2 Corn on the cob 75 g (3 oz) butter Salt and pepper	1 Remove the husk and silk from the corn. Wash.	1 Place in a pan half-full of boiling unsalted water. 2 Cook for 10-12 minutes. Drain.	Sprinkle with salt and pepper. Serve with butter.

DESSERTS: Baked apples

INGREDIENTS

1 apple for each serving

25g (1 oz) raisins
1 tablespoonful
golden syrup } *for each apple*
2 tablespoonfuls
water

Preparation time,
10 minutes.

Cooking time,
30–40 minutes.

1 Wash apple, then (using an apple corer or potato peeler) remove core.

2 Make a cut in the apple skin around the centre and from this cut into the skin towards the top all the way round.

3 Place apples in an oven-proof dish.

4 Fill empty centre with raisins and syrup.

5 Place water around the apples, cover dish and bake at Gas Mark 5 (electricity 375°F/190°C) for 30–40 minutes depending on size, until just soft (test by pushing knife into centre).

To serve, remove skin from top half.

Chocolate pie

Preparation and cooking time, 20 minutes

INGREDIENTS	EQUIPMENT
100 g (4 oz) digestive biscuits	*18 cm (7 in) cake tin*
50 g (2 oz) butter	*or shallow dish*
25 g (1 oz) cornflour	*Small basin*
25 g (1 oz) sugar	*Small pan*
1 level tablespoonful cocoa	*Wooden spoon*
25 g (1 oz) butter	*Mixing bowl*
250 ml (½ pint) milk	*Rolling pin*

1 Crush biscuits in a small basin with the end of the rolling pin.

2 Melt 50 g (2 oz) butter in the pan over a low heat. Stir into crushed biscuits, mix together. Press into the base of the dish, to make pie base.

3 Place the cornflour, sugar, cocoa and butter in the pan, and gradually stir in the milk. Heat gently, stirring all the time, to boiling and boil for 1 minute.

4 Pour onto biscuit base, and leave to cool.

If liked, decorate top with cream and grated chocolate before serving.

Fruit fool

INGREDIENTS
Small tin of fruit
250 ml (½ pint) milk
25 g (1 oz) sugar
25 g (1 oz) cornflour

Preparation and cooking time,
10–15 minutes, plus chilling
time

1 Place fruit in a bowl and mash well with fork.

2 Blend cornflour and sugar together in a basin with a little milk.

3 Heat remaining milk until almost boiling then pour onto blended ingredients, mixing well. Return to pan and boil for 1 minute.

4 Mix fruit into sauce, and chill.

If liked a few drops of food colouring can be added. Fruit fool can be served in individual dishes with extra fruit and cream for decoration.

Strawberry flummery

Preparation time, 15 minutes, setting time, 1½ hours

INGREDIENTS
1 strawberry jelly
2 eggs
50 g (2 oz) caster sugar

EQUIPMENT
Wooden spoon
Small pan
Mixing bowl
Whisk
Serving dishes
Tablespoon

1 Make jelly and put in a cool place to begin setting.

2 Separate yolks from whites of eggs.

3 Whisk yolks with 25 g (1 oz) of sugar and 2 tablespoonfuls of water, until thick and creamy.

4 Gradually whisk the cold jelly into the yolk mixture. Leave in a cold place until just beginning to set.

5 Wash and dry whisk. Whisk the egg whites until very stiff. Whisk in remaining 25 g (1 oz) of sugar.

6 Whisk into the almost setting jelly.

7 Pour into serving dishes and leave in a cold place to set.

Apple Charlotte

A quick inexpensive dessert

Preparation and cooking time, 20 minutes

INGREDIENTS

2 cooking apples	*3 slices of bread*
1 tablespoonful golden syrup	*50 g (2 oz) butter*
1 tablespoonful marmalade	*1 tablespoonful sugar*
	Top of the milk (or single cream)

1 Peel, core and slice the apples.

2 Place the syrup and the marmalade in a pan, and add the apple slices. Stir over a low heat until the apples are soft.

3 Remove crusts from the bread and cut the bread into even-sized cubes.

4 Melt butter in a small heavy frying pan over a low heat, add the bread and fry gently until just brown. Turn off the heat and stir in the sugar.

5 Place the apples in the base of two small dishes and top with the bread cubes.

6 Serve with the top of the milk or single cream.

Yogurt

Preparation time, 15 minutes

INGREDIENTS
1 pint U.H.T.
(Long Life) milk
1 tablespoonful
natural yogurt

EQUIPMENT
Vacuum flask

1 Make sure that all equipment to be used is very clean (either by boiling or by using sterilising liquid or tablets).

2 Warm vacuum flask.

3 Heat milk to 110°F (43°C) – warm.

4 Add fresh yogurt.

5 Pour into vacuum flask. Close securely and leave 8–10 hours to set.

6 Remove from flask by shaking. Put in a covered container and refrigerate until needed.

Yogurt can be served plain and either sweetened or natural; a thin honey can be mixed in; any prepared fruit can be added; for slimmers, saccharin dissolved in a little water can be used to sweeten.

ENTERTAINING

MENU

Smoked mackerel pâté
(or Quick egg mayonnaise)

Speciality chicken
or Kebabs with Barbecue Sauce
or Moussaka)

Fresh fruit salad
(or Orange and grape creams)

Smoked mackerel pâté

INGREDIENTS

*1 fillet cooked
smoked mackerel
(100–125 g : 4–5 oz)
75 g (3 oz) butter – Parsley
1 lemon – Pepper – Toast
Cucumber – Lettuce*

Preparation time, 15 minutes

1 Place mackerel in a small pan with a close-fitting lid, add 3 tablespoonfuls water and heat gently to boiling point.

2 Reduce heat and poach for 3–4 minutes. Test, using a pointed knife.

3 Meanwhile, cut lemon in half. Squeeze juice from one half. Wash and tear lettuce. Thinly slice cucumber.

4 Drain fish, and flake flesh. Discard skin and any bones. Mix fish with butter, lemon juice and pepper until very smooth. Place in a small dish, and chill.

5 Serve with lemon wedges, lettuce, sliced tomato and toast.

A very economical starter with an individual taste.

Quick egg mayonnaise

Preparation time, 15 minutes

INGREDIENTS

2 eggs
A few lettuce leaves
3–4 tablespoonfuls mayonnaise
Cayenne pepper

1 Hard-boil eggs for 10 minutes, then cool quickly.

2 Wash lettuce, and make a bed of lettuce leaves on two small plates.

3 Shell and cut eggs in half lengthways.

4 Place eggs cut side down, cover with mayonnaise, and sprinkle with cayenne pepper.

5 Serve.

Speciality chicken (for 4)

Preparation and cooking time, 40–45 minutes

INGREDIENTS

4 chicken joints
2 rashers bacon
100 g (4 oz) prawns or shrimps
1 large red pepper (chop and de-seed)
1 large onion
1 teaspoonful chopped dried parsley
Salt and pepper
100 g (4 oz) peas
2 chicken stock cubes
200 g (8 oz) long grain rice
100 g (4 oz) butter
Small tin of pineapple pieces
100 g (4 oz) mushrooms

EQUIPMENT

Chopping board
Small sharp knife
Frying pan
Large pan

1. Place chicken joints in frying pan with 25 g (1 oz) butter, salt and pepper. Cook gently for 15–20 minutes.

2. Add chopped bacon, onion and pepper, and fry a further 5 minutes.

3. Place 1 litre (2 pints) of water in a pan, and bring to boil with 1 teaspoonful salt. Add rice, peas and pepper, and cook for 10 minutes.

4. Add crumbled stock cubes to frying pan, together with parsley and sliced mushrooms. Drain rice and peas.

5. Remove chicken from pan – keep warm. Add remaining butter to pan and when melted add drained rice and remaining ingredients. Fry gently for 5 minutes.

6. Pile rice mixture into dish, top with chicken and serve with a green salad.

Kebabs with Barbecue sauce

Preparation and cooking time, 40–45 minutes

Kebabs are small pieces of meat and vegetables served on a long skewer. Usually one kebab is served for each person.

INGREDIENTS
for each person:
Cooking oil or melted butter (1–2 tablespoonfuls)
Salt and pepper
1 or 2 2.5 cm (1 inch) cubes of lean lamb, steak or pork
1 rolled piece of streaky bacon
1–2 mushrooms – wash
1–2 pieces lamb's kidneys
1 small sausage (cut in 2)
1 small tomato
1–2 small onions or slices of onion

1 Prepare all the above ingredients, and dip in oil or melted butter. Sprinkle with salt and pepper, and arrange on a grill rack on long kebab skewers.

2 Pre-heat grill and cook on a moderate heat, turning once or twice, for 10–15 minutes until meat is cooked.

Barbecue sauce

Preparation and cooking time, 30 minutes

INGREDIENTS

25 g (1 oz) butter
1 medium onion
(finely chopped or grated)
25 g (1 oz) plain flour
125 ml ($\frac{1}{4}$ pint) water
4 tablespoonfuls vinegar
1 tablespoonful
Worcestershire sauce
Juice of 1 lemon
125 ml ($\frac{1}{4}$ pint) tomato
ketchup
2 tomatoes skinned and
chopped
1 teaspoonful made mustard
50 g (2 oz) brown sugar
$\frac{1}{2}$ teaspoonful salt

1 Melt the butter over a low heat, add the onion, cover pan and cook gently until just soft.

2 Stir in the flour, gradually add the water and the remaining ingredients, then bring slowly to the boil, stirring all the time.

3 Lower the heat, cover, and simmer for 20 minutes.

Serve with kebabs and boiled rice.

Moussaka (for 2)

Preparation time, 20 minutes,
cooking time, 1 hour

INGREDIENTS

1 medium aubergine
2 tablespoonfuls cooking oil
*2 medium onions – peeled
and sliced*
200 g (8 oz) minced beef
2 tomatoes – skinned
*125 ml ($\frac{1}{4}$ pint) stock (1 stock
cube plus 125 ml ($\frac{1}{4}$ pint) water)*
2 tablespoonfuls tomato sauce
4 tablespoonfuls top of the milk
Salt and pepper – 1 egg

1 Wash (peel if wished) and slice the aubergine thinly and
   fry in the oil for 4–5 minutes, then add salt and pepper

2 Arrange half in the base of the oven-proof dish, put
   remainder on plate at one side.

3 Using same pan, lightly fry the minced beef for 4–5
   minutes, then put on plate meantime.

4 Fry onions (in same pan) until just soft and brown.

5 Arrange layers of minced beef and onion on top of the
   aubergines.

6 Top with sliced tomatoes, and remaining aubergine.

7 Mix the stock and tomato sauce together, pour into dish

8 Bake for 30 minutes at Gas Mark 4 (electricity
   350°F/180°C).

9 Beat together egg and top of the milk, with more salt and pepper, pour into dish.

10 Bake for a further 15–20 minutes until sauce is set and golden brown.

If entertaining, the first stages up to 7 can be made in advance.

Moussaka may be served with additional vegetables and potatoes.

Fresh fruit salad (for 4)

INGREDIENTS

Preparation time, 30 minutes

1 orange
50g (2 oz) grapes
(green or black)
1 red skinned apple
1 banana
1 pear
Any other fruit in season
Juice and rind of 1 lemon
100g (4 oz) sugar
200 ml ($\frac{1}{3}$ pint) water

1 Wash lemon, then thinly pare off the rind, using a vegetable peeler. Place rind in a small pan with the water and sugar. Bring to the boil, then leave to infuse until cold.

2 Prepare fruit in the order given above. Place in serving dish and squeeze lemon juice over.

3 Strain syrup over fruit, turning the fruit over to cover.

Serve on day of preparation with cream or top of the milk.

Countdown for meal served at 8 pm

6 pm
Set the table.
Make the table decoration.
Prepare lettuce and tomato for pâté.

6.25
Make the syrup for the fruit salad – chill.
Make pâté – chill.

6.50
Complete the fruit salad and place in a serving dish.

Orange and grape creams (for 2)

INGREDIENTS

*1 rounded teaspoonful of
powdered gelatine*
1 tablespoonful water
1 carton yogurt (orange)
7 tablespoonfuls double cream

Topping
*1 level tablespoonful lemon
curd – 25 g (1 oz) grapes
(black or green)*
Juice of ½ lemon

Preparation time, 20 minutes,
plus chilling time

1 Place water in a small bowl, over a pan of hot water. Add
   gelatine, and stir until dissolved. Heat gently if necessary.

2 Place yogurt in mixing bowl, and whisk in the gelatine.

3 Whisk cream until stiff, then whisk gently into yogurt.

4 Pour into two glasses or dishes and chill.

5 Wash and halve grapes, and remove pips.

6 Mix lemon curd with lemon juice, pile grapes on top of
   orange yogurt mixture, and pour lemon glaze over. Serve.

7.10
Get out the
ingredients for the
chicken dish –
prepare where
necessary.
Cook the chicken.
Place salad on
plates for pâté.
Slice lemon. Make
toast.

7.35
Complete the
chicken dish.
Check the table.
Remember serving
spoons, salt and
pepper etc.

8 pm
Serve the meal.
If there is any need
for delay, cover the
chicken dish
completely in foil
and keep hot in a
warm oven.

OTHER MENU IDEAS

Moussaka
Fresh fruit salad

Easy chicken savoury
Green beans or carrots
Baked potatoes
Chocolate pie

Lemon baked fish
Tomatoes
Peas
Potato croquettes
Fruit in jelly

Liver Risotto
Fruit fool

Mixed vegetable soup
Savoury liver
Creamed potatoes
Sprouts
Gravy
Baked apples
Custard or icecream

Corned beef hash
Assorted pickles
Fresh fruit

Leek and ham au gratin
Potato croquettes
Fresh fruit salad

Quick egg mayonnaise
Kebabs and barbecue sauce
Orange and grape creams

TABLE LAYOUT & DECORATION

The way that food is presented is very important, and presentation does not have to be elaborate or expensive.

If it is well thought out it can be very effective.

The general colour of the meal can be emphasized and enhanced for example by using coloured paper napkins and a simple flower or leaf arrangement.

MAKE WATER~LILY NAPKINS!

1 *Open out napkin on a flat surface and fold the four corners to the centre.*

2 *Fold the (newly made) four corners to the centre.*

3 *Carefully turn over and again fold the four corners to the centre. You should end up with a 100 mm or 125 mm square (4 or 5 inches).*

4 *Place a tumbler in the centre of this square to anchor it, and gently pull up each corner from the* underside.

5 *Go round again and pull up four small flaps on the underside situated between each folded-up corner. This will curve the lily towards the glass and keep the shape when the glass is removed.*

A centrepiece can be made of the cheeseboard by adding leaves and grapes.

The white linen tablecloth is definitely no longer necessary: attractive tablemats save time and effort and introduce informality.

For candlelit suppers, use firmly-placed candles in empty bottles or use the idea of wax floating in water in large glasses.

Index